Contents

KU-649-252

Words appearing in the text in bold, **like this**, are explained in the Glossary.

The Victorian age

✤ ✤

The Victorian age is named after Queen Victoria. She became Britain's queen in 1837 and reigned until her death in 1901. She was the world's most famous woman in an age when men, rather than women, dominated. All Britain's prime ministers and **Members of Parliament** were men. During the Victorian age, Britain became the richest and most powerful nation in the world. The **British Empire** included a quarter of the world's land and people.

Victorian Britain

Britain's population more than doubled in the 19th century, from 15 million in 1801 to over 37 million by 1901. People moved from the country to live and work in fast-growing industrial towns and cities. These changes had a great effect on women's lives. The **Industrial Revolution** created new work for women. For many it brought hard labour, but for some it offered an opportunity to become independent.

Victorians were proud of the British Empire, which was ruled by Queen Victoria. This map from the time shows the countries of the empire in red.

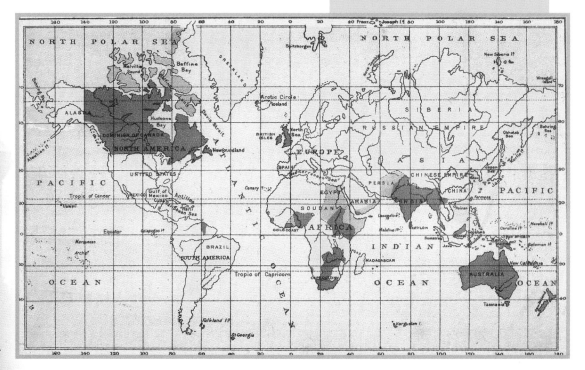

Victorian Women

Brenda Williams

Heinemann
LIBRARY

www.heinemann.co.uk/library
Visit our website to find out more information about **Heinemann Library** books.

To order:
 Phone 44 (0) 1865 888066
Send a fax to 44 (0) 1865 314091
Visit the Heinemann Bookshop at www.heinemann.co.uk/library to browse our catalogue and order online.

First published in Great Britain by Heinemann Library, Halley Court, Jordan Hill, Oxford OX2 8EJ, part of Harcourt Education.

Heinemann is a registered trademark of Harcourt Education Ltd.

© Harcourt Education Ltd 2003
The moral right of the proprietor has been asserted.

All rights reserved. No part of this publication may be reproduced, stored in a retrieval system, or transmitted in any form or by any means, electronic, mechanical, photocopying, recording, or otherwise, without either the prior written permission of the publishers or a licence permitting restricted copying in the United Kingdom issued by the Copyright Licensing Agency Ltd, 90 Tottenham Court Road, London W1T 4LP (www.cla.co.uk).

Editorial: Lucy Thunder and Helen Cox
Design: Jo Hinton-Malivoire, Richard Parker and Tinstar Design Limited (www.tinstar.co.uk)
Picture Research: Rebecca Sodergren
Production: Séverine Ribierre

Originated by Ambassador Litho Ltd
Printed in Hong Kong, China
    by Wing King Tong

ISBN 0 431 14624 1
07 06 05 04 03
10 9 8 7 6 5 4 3 2 1

British Library Cataloguing in Publication Data
Williams, Brenda
    Victorian Women. – (People in the past)
    305.4'0941'09034
A full catalogue record for this book is available from the British Library.

Acknowledgements
The publishers would like to thank the following for permission to reproduce photographs: Beamish Museum p. **42**; Billie Love Historical Collection pp. **6**, **12**, **16**, **23**; Hulton Getty pp. **22**, **25**, **29**; Mary Evans Picture Library pp. **5**, **7**, **8**, **10**, **13**, **14**, **15**, **17**, **18**, **19**, **20**, **24**, **26**, **27**, **31**, **32**, **35**, **37**, **40**; National Portrait Gallery p. **38**; Victoria and Albert Museum p. **21**.

Cover photograph of Victorian flowersellers reproduced with permission of Hulton Getty.

The publishers would like to thank Rebecca Vickers for her assistance with the preparation of this book.

Every effort has been made to contact copyright holders of any material reproduced in this book. Any omissions will be rectified in subsequent printings if notice is given to the publishers.

PUBLIC LIBRARIES
46670
644784   SCH
J942.081

Victorian Britain went through startling changes. Women were part of this **revolution**. Many of them did new jobs in factories.

Rich and poor women

There were three basic classes, or groups, in Victorian society. At the bottom were the **working classes**, which included women such as servants or factory workers. **Middle-class** women included teachers, shopkeepers and those whose husbands were farmers, skilled **craftworkers** or office workers. At the top of society were the richest, the **upper classes**. These included the aristocracy (women with titles such as Duchess) and the wives of wealthy businessmen or factory-owners.

Women in a changing world

Victorian women lived through startling changes brought about by new technology. At the start of the century, nothing travelled faster than a galloping horse. By the 1840s, a young woman might have taken her first exciting ride on a steam train, and by the 1850s had her photograph taken. As an older woman, in the 1890s, she may have talked to a friend on the telephone, danced to a **gramophone** and ridden in a motor car.

In this book, you will learn more about women in Victorian times, both rich and poor. You will explore their lives at home, at work and at play. Next time you look at an old photo of a Victorian family, you may feel you know the women in the picture a little better.

Victorian money

In Victorian times people counted up their money in pounds (£), shillings (s) and pennies (d). There were 20 shillings in 1 pound, and 12 pennies in 1 shilling. A woman spent 3d (just over 1p) a week on potatoes to feed a family of five.

5

The ideal woman

The kind of life a Victorian woman led depended on whether or not she had to go out to work to help raise her family. **Upper-class** and **middle-class** women usually did not work. **Working-class** women often did.

In Victorian Britain, most people knew their place. That means they knew which class (group) they had been born into, and they expected to stay there. It was possible to climb the social ladder, but easier to slide down it. Working-class women could marry above them (a maid might marry her employer). A woman who married beneath her (by becoming the wife of her coachman, for instance) risked being an **outcast** in society.

How Victorians saw women

Many Victorian men – and women – from the upper and middle classes believed a woman's place was in the home. The ideal woman made a comfortable home for her husband and looked after her children.

Women were expected to be good, patient and modest. Some men seem to have thought of women as angels and were shocked when they behaved like people! Some men talked about new ideas with their wives and daughters, or discussed business and politics with them. However, most men did not expect women to have ideas of their own.

The 'ideal' woman was pictured in paintings and statues. The ideal Victorian woman ran her home without fuss, leaving her husband to worry about the wider world.

The heroine of the storm

Grace Darling was the ideal of a Victorian heroine, brave but modest. She was the daughter of a lighthouse keeper in the Farne Islands, off the Northumberland coast. In 1838, aged 22, she rowed through a storm in a small fishing boat with her father to rescue survivors from a wrecked steamship, the *Forfarshire*. A shy girl, Grace became a celebrity. She was honoured in poems and paintings, and received hundreds of letters and visitors. She died at the age of 26.

Women were considered 'the weaker sex'. This was quite untrue of course. Many men were taught to treat women with respect and politeness, and to take care of them. Some independent women showed they could look after themselves, but most women accepted their role without argument.

Women who broke the mould

Many Victorian women spent their lives being daughter, housewife and mother within a family. A few broke out of this mould, to live alone. Others earned their own living, became teachers or scientists, or made dangerous journeys alone in foreign countries. On the whole, however, most women did not have much opportunity for adventure.

Grace Darling's bravery challenged the idea of women as timid and physically weak. The fact that she was so quiet and shy increased people's admiration of her courage.

Growing up

❖ ❖

Many Victorian girls started work at the age of ten or even younger. They helped with jobs at home or on the farm, and looked after the smaller children. By this age, many girls knew how to run a family.

Some richer families paid a **governess** to live in their home and teach their children. Lessons for the girls included maths (for checking household bills), drawing, singing, piano, the Bible, posture (walking and sitting properly) and sewing. Some girls learned a little French, too.

In the early 19th century, parents who could afford a few pennies a week sent their daughters to a 'dame school'. The 'dame' was like a child-minder who taught children to add up, to read and to write a little. At home, mothers taught girls to cook, sew, clean and keep house. **Middle-class** girls learned to read, write and keep household **accounts**.

They were also taught ladylike 'accomplishments', such as singing, drawing or music. They were shown how to walk properly, make polite conversation and give orders to servants. This prepared them for married life.

Girls at school

Until about 1850, most girls who had lessons were taught in their own or somebody else's home. A few were sent away to school. In the 1820s and 1830s, the three Brontë sisters (Charlotte, Emily and Anne) went to **boarding school**. Charlotte was eight years old when she first went away to Cowan Bridge School, where the oldest of her fellow pupils was 22. The Yorkshire school cost £14 a year, but Charlotte hated it. The three Brontë girls all later became famous writers.

Better schools were needed, to give girls the same chances as boys. The first training college for women teachers opened in 1848. By the 1850s, improved schools for girls were being run by **pioneer** teachers such as Frances Mary Buss and Dorothea Beale. Their belief that education was important created a new generation of career women, as some of their pupils became teachers, doctors and lawyers. However, it was 1880 before the law said that all girls must go to primary school, and only after 1891 was schooling free.

For most girls, a career was not an option. They expected – and most looked forward to – marriage and homemaking.

The joys of school life

Charlotte Brontë hated the food at her school. The porridge was burnt and had 'offensive fragments' of other things in it. Rice puddings were boiled in water taken from a rain barrel. A meat and potato pie, served on Saturdays, was made from the week's leftovers! At the strictest schools, girls were forced to wear very stiff 'stays' (metal-framed **corsets**) to make them sit up straight.

Marriage

✤ ✤

Courtship, engagement, marriage and **widowhood** were the landmarks in many women's lives. Most Victorian women expected to get married and raise children. Once married, a wife and her husband expected to stay married until death parted them. **Divorce** was expensive, and very rare.

Meeting the right partner

Some families tried **matchmaking**, to find suitable husbands for their daughters. Popular books such as *Hints for Husband-Catching or A Manual for Marriageable Misses* (1846) gave tips on how to find a husband. Young men and women often met by being introduced by family or friends. It was thought wrong for a girl to make the first move. At a dance, she had to wait for a partner to invite her to join in. It was the custom for girls to fill in a card with the names of the young men they had agreed to dance with. A popular girl might be fully booked before the first dance had ended.

A good marriage was important in Victorian middle-class life. This picture shows the bride cutting the wedding cake at the family celebration. The wedding ceremony would have taken place in church. A maidservant (right) pours coffee for the guests.

Choosing a husband

Girls enjoyed traditional games to find out whom they might marry. They would spin a Bible tied around a girl's **garter**, while repeating the alphabet. The last letter spoken as the book stopped twirling gave the first letter of the future husband's name. 'A' might mean Albert, and so on.

Courtship

Courtship meant 'walking out' as a couple, perhaps on Sunday (most people's only day off), wearing Sunday best clothes. In strict households, a girl was not left alone with her sweetheart. A sister or friend stayed with them as a chaperone (companion). The young man had to ask permission from a girl's father when he asked her to marry him. If father and daughter both said yes, the man gave the girl an engagement ring. The ring should be 'as handsome a present as he can afford to buy', wrote Mrs Humphry in *Manners for Men* (1897). Most couples married within a year of getting engaged.

The wedding

The wedding itself usually took place in a church. Guests gave presents and threw rice over the newlyweds. The man was expected to provide the home for the couple to live in, and to pay for the furniture.

In her book, Mrs Humphry warned girls that the nicest young men sadly could turn into less than perfect husbands as they grew older. 'They are late for every meal … disagreeable in their manner at home; rough to the servants, rude to their wives and irritable to their children.'

Babies, more babies

Marriage usually meant babies, and Victorian families were often large. Queen Victoria had nine children. Pregnancy could be dangerous, however. All babies were born at home, often with no doctor present. Many women died when something went wrong during the birth, or because they caught childbirth fever afterwards.

Running the household

Women kept Victorian life running smoothly, by managing the home. In the **census** of 1851, the term 'housewife' was used as a job title for the first time in Britain. The Victorian mother looked after her children, usually without much help from her husband. She directed the servants, if there were any. She went shopping, kept the house clean and fed the family. Many women managed the household **accounts**, paying bills out of the housekeeping money given them by their husbands. Women also acted as family nurse whenever anyone was sick. Home was the woman's world – but the husband was its master.

New gadgets to buy

In 1879, an American named Julia McNair Wright wrote: 'It is the duty of the husband to make money and of the wife to spend it judiciously [carefully]'. Eager to learn new ways of doing things, young women turned to books. They read Isabella Beeton's *Book of Household Management* (see page 15) and Mrs Wright's housewives' encyclopedia, *The Complete Home*. Books like these encouraged better-off women to buy new **gadgets**, such as mechanical washtubs, iceboxes and carpet sweepers. However, most homes had to manage without these new inventions.

In a comfortable **middle-class** home, the woman was expected to give daily orders to the servants. She spoke to the cook, for example, to make sure that dinner was ordered for the family and any guests that evening.

The writer John Ruskin (1819-1900) called home a place of 'peace and shelter', but home life was not always tranquil. Some men treated their wives like unpaid servants, or even beat them. Before the 1860s, women had few rights in law. Without income (money) of their own, women had to ask their husbands for housekeeping money. Some working men did, however, and handed over their weekly wages to their wives to spend.

Making ends meet

For many poor women, life was a constant struggle. Their 'household' was not always even one room – in city **slums** two or three families often shared a room, taking turns to sleep in the beds. Things were not much better for poor country families. Overcrowded cottages meant no privacy for women or their children. Rooms were cold and damp. In winter, wet washing dripped on the floor from lines strung across the room. Women were expected to buy food and prepare meals. They managed as best they could on whatever money their husbands gave them each week, plus what little they could earn themselves.

This picture shows a poor **working-class** family at home. The woman here would have had no servants to help her. Nor could she afford the gadgets illustrated in newspaper advertisements.

13

Queen of the kitchen

The Victorian kitchen was a woman's territory. A rich woman had a cook to prepare family meals, but many Victorian women were busy in the kitchen every day. Countrywomen could pick fresh vegetables from their cottage gardens, and collect mushrooms, wild berries or nuts from the hedgerows. Townswomen had to shop for their food.

Feeding the family

The kitchen was in use from breakfast time until evening. It was one of the warmest rooms in the house, with a big iron **kitchen range** that heated an oven and a hot water tank. Poorer women often had no oven, but made do with the bare essentials – a pump for water, a sink, a table, a tiny fire and whatever food was to be bought for a few pennies. Many women factory workers had little time for cooking. They would buy cheap pies, oatcakes (oatmeal pancakes), or 'a bit of fish' from a local shop.

This advertisement shows what a large Victorian kitchen looked like. Women prepared food on the big wooden table, and cooked on the coal-burning range.

Isabella Beeton died after the birth of her fourth son in 1865, before she was 30 years old. Many women since then have followed her cookery advice.

Countrywomen made the main meal in the evening when men came home from work. Often it would be bacon, cut from a side of meat that was hung from the ceiling. It was cooked with cabbage or peas, potatoes, and a 'roly poly' pudding wrapped in a cloth. All this was boiled together in one big pot, with the vegetables in nets.

Fresh food, bubbling away

The Victorian housewife had no refrigerator, so most food was bought fresh. She spent a lot of time preparing meals – making pastry, peeling potatoes, skinning rabbits or plucking chickens. Many women set aside one day a week for baking bread. In poor homes, many housewives kept a pot of stew heating over the fire, adding fresh vegetables and whatever scraps of meat they could buy.

Mrs Beeton's household hints

Isabella Mayson became famous as 'Mrs Beeton'. Her name appears on cookery books still used today. To help get over the death of her first baby in 1857, she wrote her *Book of Household Management*. The ingredients for her Christmas pudding recipe cost 4s (20p) for eight people. It would be more economical, she wrote, to make five or six puddings at one time. Mrs Beeton liked a tidy kitchen: 'A place for everything and everything in its place', she wrote.

Lady of the house

No matter how big the home, the lady of the house was expected to run things. Rich women and many **middle-class** women had servants to do the housework. A middle-class family might have just one servant-girl, or maid. A wealthy family living in a big town house or a country mansion would have a small army of servants.

Left in charge

The lady of the house gave orders to the servants while her husband was away at work. She told the cook what dishes to prepare for dinner in the evening. She made sure that beds were made, carpets swept, and shelves dusted. The mistress of the house would also oversee what the gardener was doing, and pick fresh flowers to make the home sweet-smelling and attractive. Small children were often left in the care of a **nanny**. This left time to do other things. Wealthy Victorian women did not go to keep-fit classes, take foreign holidays or do part-time jobs. They spent time visiting friends, or shopping in town. Others took up hobbies, such as painting or studying local history. Women at home read books, did embroidery and wrote letters to friends. Some just spent the day feeling bored.

This Victorian illustration shows the lady of the house instructing the cook.

Visiting cards and etiquette

A lady welcomed visitors 'at home', usually between 4 and 7 p.m. Lady Blenkinsop, for example, lived in a large town house. If she did not wish to see anyone, her servant would tell a caller: 'Her Ladyship is not at home'. The visitor would leave her visiting card. On another day, Lady Blenkinsop might return the call and leave her own card. Respectable ladies followed certain rules of behaviour, known as etiquette. Most would not receive men (other than relatives) alone at home, for fear of gossip.

Good works

Some rich women put their spare time to good use. They visited elderly, poor or sick people, taking gifts of food or clothes. They organized committees to raise money for poor children or for church work overseas. Some women studied or travelled. Marianne North was rich and single. She became an expert on plants, travelling the world to study and paint flowers. A few rich women campaigned for **women's rights**.

A well-to-do lady visits a poor family. Rich people were expected to help those less fortunate than themselves. Giving them money, food or unwanted clothes was known as charity.

Working women

Poor women in Victorian times worked to earn money for **rent** and food. They often toiled in factories, mills and farms for long hours and little money. Richer women did not have to work, if they had a husband to provide a home for them.

Women's toil

Many women with jobs in factories or on farms started work as children. Girls mended broken threads on spinning frames or carried clay moulds to the kilns (ovens) in potteries. Until a new law stopped it in 1842, women and girls had worked underground in coal mines. On farms, women did heavy work such as clearing fields of stones and picking potatoes. Many thousands of women worked as household servants (see page 28).

Unlike today, there were no **pensions**, so women worked until they were old. The writer W H Hudson, in his book *A Shepherd's Life* (1910), told the story of an old woman in Wiltshire who called at a farm seeking work. The farmer and his wife gave her a job scaring crows away from a field of swedes. They gave her an old hat, coat and rusty gun, and she spent her days sitting in the open fields. Most working women were poorly paid and worked from dawn until dusk. The Ten-Hour **Act** of 1847 was supposed to stop women working more than 10 hours a day, but many still did so.

Some women were employed as typists, a job that – though not well paid – gave many young women a first taste of independence.

18

New jobs for women

In 1851, the **census** showed that there were only nineteen women clerks (office workers) in the whole of Britain. By 1881, this number had risen to 7000 and ten years later to 22,000. Many of these new women office workers were using **typewriters**.

New and larger shops also provided jobs for women. Shop work was cleaner and safer than working in a factory.

Getting to work

New jobs meant more women workers travelling to work by horse-bus and by train. Train companies provided women-only waiting rooms and women-only compartments on trains. The first woman waiting-room attendant started work at London's Paddington Station in 1838, when the new Great Western Railway opened. Edinburgh had three women booking clerks as early as 1858.

A match for the strikers

In 1888, women making matches went on **strike** to protest at being paid just 4 shillings (20p) for working 60 hours a week. It was unusual then for women workers to protest in this way. The **campaigner** Annie Besant helped them to organize a strike in the match factory. Annie and Charles Bradlaugh, with whom she lived but did not marry (a scandal in Victorian times), campaigned for **socialism**.

Annie Besant fought for the rights of the match girls. The girls shown here were some of the 1400 match girls who went on strike in 1888 at the Bryant and May match factory.

Clothes

Most Victorian clothes look heavy and uncomfortable to us today. Many were made from wool, which was warm but thick and difficult to wash. When factories began making cheap cotton dresses, women found them easier to wash and dry. Cotton clothes could also be dyed in bright colours.

Hoops and hour-glass figures

By the 1850s, well off fashionable women were wearing a bell-shaped skirt called a crinoline, which was held in shape by a hooped frame. Crinolines went out of style by 1870, and the fullness shifted to the back of the skirt where it formed a sticking-out bump, called a bustle. In the 1890s, the fashion changed again, to more tight-fitting dresses.

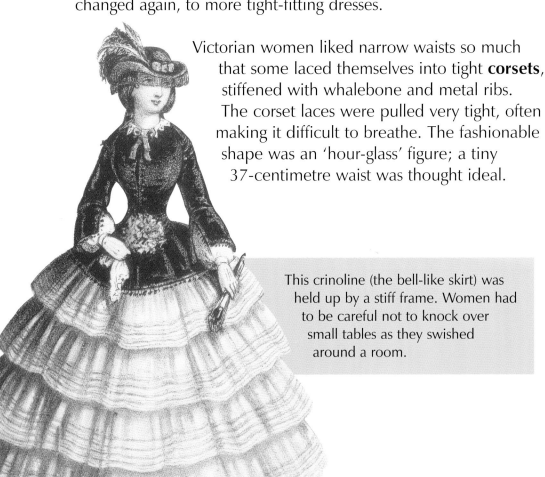

Victorian women liked narrow waists so much that some laced themselves into tight **corsets**, stiffened with whalebone and metal ribs. The corset laces were pulled very tight, often making it difficult to breathe. The fashionable shape was an 'hour-glass' figure; a tiny 37-centimetre waist was thought ideal.

This crinoline (the bell-like skirt) was held up by a stiff frame. Women had to be careful not to knock over small tables as they swished around a room.

This illustration from the 1890s shows fashionable women wearing skirts with bustles. The little girl's skirt is a miniature version of the adult ones.

Keeping snug and dressing up

A Victorian woman who could afford it would wear lots of layers. First she put on lace-trimmed drawers (long pants), then an under petticoat, a starched (stiffened) petticoat, a softer muslin (thin cotton) petticoat and finally the dress. In winter, some women wore 'combinations' of woollen vest and woollen drawers. Cheap cotton underwear went on sale from the 1870s.

Most people bought cheap factory-made clothes, or made their own at home. Richer women went to smart fashion stores, to pick out a material and style, and be measured. Then a dressmaker made the dress. The Victorians seldom threw away old clothes. Unwanted garments were given to servants or sold to second-hand shops.

Working clothes

Women servants usually wore a cap and apron. A few women doing heavy work outdoors wore trousers, but this was unusual. In cold weather, women put on woollen shawls – few poor women had a winter coat. To keep their feet dry, some countrywomen wore wooden pattens (undershoes). Factory workers wore wooden slip-on shoes called clogs. Women waterproofed boots by rubbing melted candlewax into the leather.

Black for mourning

Victorians wore dark clothes when they were in **mourning**. A **widow** wore black after the death of her husband. Queen Victoria wore mourning dress for 40 years following the death in 1861 of her husband, Prince Albert. If a family wedding took place during the mourning period, the bride wore grey or lavender, not white.

Hair, hats and jewels

Hair care could take almost as long as getting dressed. Many women, rich or poor, were proud of 'a wealth of hair' worn very long and kept in place with pins. Thick corkscrew curls and ringlets were fashionable before about 1850. Then a rather severe centre parting became the favoured style, with a bun or knot of long hair gathered at the back. Fringes were fashionable from the 1880s.

Women washed their hair in ordinary soap, using natural plant oils and dyes to make it shiny and smell nice. Shampoos first became popular in the 1890s. Without electric hairdriers, women towel-rubbed their hair dry in front of a coal fire.

Women wore large, pretty hats in summer. This kept them cool and protected their skin from the sun. Parasols also helped. Men always took off their hats indoors, but women could keep hats on while visiting friends.

Hats for all weathers

Men and women wore hats whenever they were out of doors. To be sunburnt was thought unladylike, so rich and poor women wore bonnets on a hot summer days. Richer women carried umbrellas on rainy days, and **parasols** to shade them on sunny days. Hats with brims, including straw hats, became fashionable in the 1890s.

Bonnets were often tied in place by ribbons. Long hatpins were very popular by the 1890s, allowing women to tilt their hats at jaunty angles without having them blown off by the wind. Bold young women of the late 1890s wore thin face-veils and scarves tied under their chins to keep their hats on when riding in open-topped motor cars.

A bird on the hat

In 1866 a fashion writer in the *Illustrated Times* newspaper joked that to make a hat, a woman need only: 'Take a piece of plaited straw…and bend it into any shape you please so long as you can balance the article on top of your head.' By the 1880s, some rich women wore hats decorated with feathers, fruit, flowers and insects. The Society for the Protection of Birds, founded in 1889, complained of the number of rare birds' feathers and even whole stuffed birds on women's hats.

Sparkling for a party

Poor women bought jewellery made from cheap metal and glass, or made their own from wooden or clay beads. For parties and balls, wealthy women displayed expensive jewels on their hair, neck and arms. They wore tight necklaces called chokers around the neck and thick bracelets on their arms. Pinned to their dresses were brooches made from gold or silver, set with diamonds, rubies and other precious stones. A black stone called jet was popular, as it could be worn by women in **mourning**. Very rich women wore pearls in strings as necklaces, in large drop earrings, and in **tiaras** set alongside sparkling diamonds.

Much Victorian jewellery was elaborate and rather heavy. Women still wear similar items, like pearls and chokers, today.

23

Having fun

Many **working-class** women had little time free from work and so made the best of their days off. A servant girl might enjoy a day in the park, at the fair, or spend her hard-earned money on a day trip to the seaside. Women with time for leisure at home might play cards, do needlework or tend the garden. There were sporting women, too. They enjoyed archery, horse-riding (women sat side-saddle), cycling, ice-skating and roller-skating. Women also played tennis, badminton, croquet and golf. Some even went mountain climbing.

A day at the seaside

Some rich women visited France, Italy or Greece to see the sights, or went to the Swiss Alps for winter sports. For most Victorians, however, the British seaside was their playground. By the 1870s, trains were bringing holidaymakers from towns to new seaside resorts such as Blackpool and Margate. Even on a hot day at the seaside, women kept all their clothes on, carrying **parasols** to shield them from the sun. Few went into the sea, though sea bathing was believed to be healthy.

Women bathers wore heavy bathing dresses that became even heavier when soaking wet. It was an effort to swim far in them!

A woman bather wore a thick bathing dress. She went down into the water inside a bathing machine. This was a wooden hut on wheels, pulled by a horse into the sea. Then, aided by a woman attendant, the bather dipped herself in the waves. Until the 1870s, men and boys (and some girls) had swum naked, but when more women began bathing, male swimmers had to put on bathing suits. Victorian bathing dresses were so thick and heavy that only a strong swimmer could splash far in them.

Women took to wearing split skirts or 'bloomers' for cycling, a very popular pastime in the 1890s. Bloomers gave women riders more freedom to pedal.

Women on wheels

More women began to ride bicycles but this was difficult in a skirt. Imagine clambering on to a **penny-farthing** in a long dress! By 1885, bicycles looked more like modern bikes and, with air-filled tyres, were much more comfortable to ride. Some women cyclists wore 'Rational Costume' – a man's jacket, hat and 'bloomers' (loose trousers, tucked into socks).

Bloomers a threat to men

Amelia Jenks Bloomer was an American **campaigner** for **women's rights**. She thought that changing women's dress style would make men treat them more seriously. In the 1850s she started wearing a jacket, skirt and baggy trousers fastened at the ankles. People made fun of her, for a respectable Victorian woman to wear trousers was thought shocking. By the 1890s, though, bloomers were worn by very respectable women cyclists.

Women's health

Victorian women did not expect to live into their 80s, as women do today. In the 1850s, the average life expectancy for a poor person was only seventeen years. Disease, hunger, poor **sanitation**, **slum** housing, dangerous working conditions and medicines that did not work: all took a heavy toll of human life. Many children died before they reached the age of five, from diseases such as measles or scarlet fever. Many women died in childbirth.

Paying for a cure

Working women could be injured by unsafe factory machines, or made sick by choking dust and poisonous chemicals. Few poor women could afford to pay for a doctor. Instead, they relied on traditional 'country cures' or bought cheap medicines such as Holloway's Pills, which (the makers claimed) would cure any ill.

The not so daily bath

Public health in towns was very poor until the 1850s, when new drains and water pipes were laid. Even so, few homes – rich or poor – had bathrooms until the end of the 19th century. For most women, a bath was a rare treat.

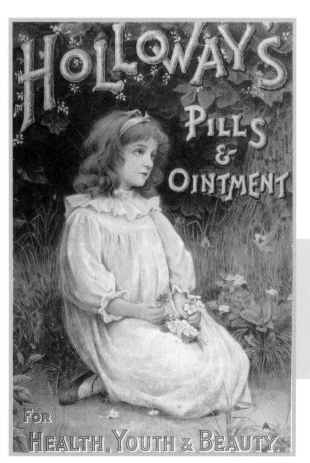

Many women nursed themselves and their families with cheap medicines. This advertisement shows a pretty young girl to make buyers think they will stay young and beautiful if they take the pills and ointment!

Whispering wisdom

Women often acted as family nurse. Countrywomen picked marsh-mallow leaves to treat boils, coltsfoot plants to make a cough medicine and put soothing dock leaves on nettle-stings and sores. They might ask a local 'wise woman' to whisper magical-sounding rhymes over the patient to charm out a thorn or remove an unsightly wart.

Many working women washed their faces and hands in the kitchen sink. Once a week, a woman might have an all-over wash, first washing the top half and then stepping into a small footbath to do the rest. Most homes still had outside toilets and there were no public toilets for women. From the mid-19th century the growth in city department stores was welcomed by women shoppers because these stores had 'retiring rooms' (lavatories). It was not until 1884 that the Ladies Lavatory Company opened the first public lavatory for women in Oxford Street, London.

Diet and exercise

Many poor women were thin and underfed. Richer women were sometimes overweight, usually because they ate too much stodgy food or sat down for too long. Yet generally, women walked more than many people do today. Many working women got their exercise walking to work, and then spent most of the day on their feet.

Women nursed relatives at home. But home nursing could do little against killer diseases such as tuberculosis, **cholera** or typhoid fever. A Liverpool doctor in 1830 treated a poor family of thirteen. Of these, twelve were sick with the disease **typhus**. Visiting the sick with gifts of nourishing food, as shown here, was a **middle-class** duty.

Women in service

'Be firm, strict, yet kind and thoughtful to your servants…', wrote Mrs Beeton in her *Book of Household Management* (see page 15). Large homes needed staff, and there were about one million women servants in the 1850s (the time that she was writing). A wealthy man whose wife had died might hire a housekeeper to run his house. Having a servant was a sign that a family was prosperous.

Cooks and housemaids

In the 1880s, a housemaid in her first job earned less than £10 a year. An experienced cook was paid up to £50 a year. A shopkeeper or a farmer might employ one maidservant. She did all the heavy work – scrubbing floors, carrying coal buckets, clearing and lighting fires, serving meals, washing-up, cleaning and dusting. If a servant girl married, she usually left her job.

Working your way up

A servant girl began at the bottom, as a **scullery** maid, and rose by stages to housemaid, parlourmaid, ladies' maid or even cook. Housemaids did the heaviest fetching, carrying and cleaning. Parlourmaids had to look smart, open the front door to visitors and serve tea to the lady of the house and her guests. In the kitchen, the cook had other servants to help – girls sent running to fetch eggs, flour, spices and butter while she mixed a cake, for example.

Invisible servants

'Upstairs' or 'above the stairs' was the part of a large house where the master and mistress lived. 'Below stairs' was for the servants (even though servants often lived at the very top of the house). Servants went into all rooms, so the family had little privacy. Maids were expected to pass through a room without speaking, unless they were spoken to. It was as if servants became 'invisible'.

Life's ups and downs

Life in a big house could be interesting. Women servants could make friends with others who shared the work and the jokes. Life could be harder for a single 'maid of all work'. Many of these girls started work as young as twelve years old. They were alone, overworked and often homesick. They could be at the mercy of an unkind master or mistress, who might half-starve them and punish them for any mistake.

Hannah Cullick was born in 1833 and began work as a maid at the age of eight. For eighteen years, from 1854 until she married in 1873, she kept diaries to tell her fiancé about her life in service. She was a good worker, and proud of it: 'a poor drudge like me is more use … than a brought-up lady … as [she] couldn't boil a 'tatoe [potato]'.

A big house could have as many as 20 servants. Many of them were women, each with their own duties in the house.

Votes for women

Women in the 19th century did not have the same **rights** as men. No Victorian women could vote for a **Member of Parliament**, and all Members of Parliament were men. Although the country had a world-famous queen, few women took part in public life. However, some independent-thinking women began to challenge old ideas about women's place in society. This was the start of the **women's rights** movement.

Spreading the word

Harriet Martineau (1802–76) travelled to America, and saw how slaves were treated there. It seemed to her that many women were little better off. In books and newspaper articles, she argued that men would treat women as equals only if women were able to live and work as independent people. This meant voting, doing the same jobs as men for the same pay and being as well educated.

Journalism helped to spread the new ideas. In 1869, Emily Faithfull (1835–95) founded an all-female printing and publishing company called the Victoria Printing Press. She edited a magazine and ran a women's discussion society. Another **pioneer** was Millicent Fawcett (1847–1929). She was the younger sister of Elizabeth Garrett (1836–1917), who overcame many obstacles to qualify as Britain's first woman doctor (see page 37). Millicent Fawcett campaigned for women's right to vote, and for more women to go to university and run their own affairs.

What women have, they can hold

The Victorian writer and thinker John Stuart Mill believed that women should be given the vote. If they were, he wrote, 'women would no longer be classed with children and lunatics, as incapable of taking care of themselves or others…' At that time women had to hand over everything they owned to their husbands when they married. In 1882, Parliament passed the Married Women's Property Act. This new law allowed women to keep their property after they married and so gave them more independence.

Millicent Fawcett was the daughter of a rich shipowner. As the wife of a Member of Parliament she met important people. She hoped that votes for women would lead to 'the womanly and domestic side of things' becoming more important in public life.

Suffragists and suffragettes

Campaigners for women's right to vote were called suffragists and suffragettes ('suffrage' means 'the right to vote'). Suffragists believed in peaceful protest. Suffragettes were prepared to break the law. The best-known suffragette leader was Mrs Emmeline Pankhurst (1858–1928), who began campaigning in Manchester in the 1880s. She later moved to London, where she helped Annie Besant organize the match girls' strike (see pages 18 and 19). Despite all their efforts, women did not get the vote on the same terms as men (at the age of 21) until 1928.

Women writers

❖ ❖

'I want to do something with the pen, since no other means of action in politics are in a woman's power,' wrote Harriet Martineau. She knew that writing was one of the best ways for women to express their ideas in a man's world. She earned money by writing books and articles for newspapers. Harriet Martineau lived with her parents. After her father died, she cared for her mother, taking in sewing jobs to make money, but writing in every spare moment.

Women writing as men

Four of the best female writers of the Victorian age at first pretended to be men. Charlotte Brontë (1816–55) called herself Currer Bell when she sent publishers her first novel, *Jane Eyre*.

This is a picture of Charlotte Brontë who wrote the book *Jane Eyre* (published in 1847). Some readers were surprised at the way in which the **governess** Jane Eyre expressed her love for her employer, Mr Rochester. They could not understand how a 'male author' could write in such a manner.

Charlotte's sisters, Emily and Anne Brontë, used the names Ellis and Acton Bell. Emily Brontë (1818–48) wrote *Wuthering Heights*, one of the greatest English novels.

Mary Ann Evans (1819–80) wrote under the name of George Eliot. She had been educated mostly at home, and after her mother died when she was fifteen, her father expected her to run the household. Later, she fell in love with a married man. The fact that she lived with him when he had not **divorced** his wife caused a great scandal.

What women wrote about

One of the first novelists to write about **working-class** people was Elizabeth Gaskell (1810–65). She saw for herself how poor families lived in Lancashire mill-towns. One of her books, *Ruth*, was burned by angry churchgoers. They were shocked by the story of a girl who had a baby before she was married.

Some women wrote stories with a 'moral', suitable for reading aloud to the family. Others wrote love stories in which women often ran away from cruel fathers or husbands. It was easier to publish books for children, because this was thought more suitable for women writers. Anna Sewell, who wrote *Black Beauty*, and Frances Hodgson Burnett (author of *The Secret Garden*) were two successful writers whose books became 'classics', still enjoyed today.

A poet who escaped

Elizabeth Barrett (1806–61) was a poet. After her mother died, her father refused to let Elizabeth leave home. From 1841, the Barretts' London house became Elizabeth's prison, which she seldom left. She was eventually rescued by the poet Robert Browning, and they married secretly in 1846. Mr Barrett refused to see his daughter again. Elizabeth wrote a poem called *Aurora Leigh* in 1857 about a woman writer's need to be free.

Women performers

Unlike today, the theatre was once thought of as a rather low form of entertainment. By the 1880s, however, it had become respectable. Women worked as **managers** as well as performers. In 1886, the writer George Moore observed that '… all women cannot marry, they cannot enlist [become soldiers], nor yet go out to the colonies and become domestic servants. So they sigh after the stage.'

Stars of the stage

Women danced in the ballet, sang in operas, acted in serious plays, and performed popular songs in the **music halls**. Some became as famous as today's film stars. They included the actresses Ellen Terry, Lillie Langtry and the Frenchwoman Sarah Bernhardt. The music-hall singer Marie Lloyd (real name, Matilda Wood, from Hoxton, East London) made her first stage appearance in 1870 at the age of fifteen.

Most famous of all Victorian actresses was Ellen Terry, who first stepped on a stage in 1856 at the age of nine. She achieved fame in the 1870s, starring opposite Henry Irving, the greatest actor of the day.

The cleverest girl on stage

The writer Charles Dickens called Marie Wilton 'the cleverest girl I have ever seen on the stage in my time'. An actor's daughter with little education, Marie borrowed £1000 to rebuild a tumbledown London theatre nicknamed the 'Dusthole'. Renamed the Prince of Wales, it became the most fashionable theatre in town. In 1867, Marie married an actor called Squire Bancroft. As managers, they made London's theatres profitable and respectable.

The Jersey Lily

Lillie Langtry was born on the Channel Island of Jersey in 1853. Her real name was Emilie Charlotte Le Breton. She was beautiful, clever and ambitious. Her first marriage to a rich yachtsman named Edward Langtry was not a success. She moved to London, where she became friends with writers, painters and the Prince of Wales. Her actress friend Sarah Bernhardt encouraged Lillie to go on the stage. As Lillie Langtry, the 'Jersey Lily', she became an international star and toured the USA, where a town was named after her.

Among serious actresses, Helena Faucit was famous for her performances in Shakespeare's plays and for never wearing a costume that showed her ankles. She was invited to visit Queen Victoria – a sign that acting had become respectable. Beautiful actresses moved easily into high society by marrying rich men. Others spent their lives working, like Lucy Vestris who was the first woman to manage a London theatre.

Lillie Langtry was a famous Victorian beauty. Many souvenirs of her, such as postcards, were sold, and could be found even in small mining towns in America's Wild West.

Women who made a difference

Victorian actresses were often cheered. Other women in public life, however, attracted ridicule as well as admiration. This was because they were **reformers** and **pioneers**. They were not afraid to risk their reputations, or even their lives, working to improve things.

Reformers

Social reformers tried to improve health, housing, education, factories and prisons. Elizabeth Fry (1780–1845) visited prisons, making the government improve the awful conditions for women behind bars. Octavia Hill (1838–1912) provided decent homes for inner-city families, buying houses, repairing them and renting them to the poor. She set up playgrounds and open spaces for children; later she helped to found the **National Trust**.

Women's talents

Probably the most famous Victorian woman (after Queen Victoria) was Florence Nightingale (1820–1910). After nursing soldiers in the **Crimean War**, she became so ill that she never appeared in public after 1857. Working from her bed, she brought about the opening of Britain's first school for nurses in 1860. Florence Nightingale knew that women's talents were wasted. She wrote, 'Why have women passion, intellect, moral activity – these three – and a place in society where not one of these three can be exercised?'

Nursing and dosing deeds

A poem in *Punch* magazine in 1856 began: 'The sick and sorry can tell the story of her nursing and dosing deeds'. The woman who inspired these verses was Mary Seacole. While Florence Nightingale organized army nursing during the Crimean War, Mary Seacole ran a hotel, kitchen and first-aid post close to the battlefield. She had come alone from her home in Jamaica to help nurse the soldiers.

Schools and jobs for women

In 1859, a group led by Jessie Boucherett and Barbara Bodichon set up the Society for the Promotion of Employment for Women. It aimed to help women get better jobs, by teaching them mathematics, for example. Emily Davies and her friend Elizabeth Garrett studied at one of the society's schools. Later, Emily **campaigned** for women to enter universities. In 1869, she helped to found a college for girls, which later became part of Cambridge University.

Elizabeth Garrett tried to study medicine in Britain, but had to go to France to complete her training in 1870. In 1872, she opened a women's hospital in London (later named the Elizabeth Garrett Anderson Hospital). She also taught at Britain's first medical school for women. The school had been founded by Sophia Jex-Blake, who overcame the sneering of male students to qualify as a doctor in 1877.

This photograph of Elizabeth Garrett was taken in 1866. Not only was she a pioneering woman doctor, but she was also the first woman mayor in Britain. She was Millicent Fawcett's sister.

Queen Victoria

✤ ❖ ✤ ❖ ✤ ❖ ✤ ❖ ✤ ❖ ✤ ❖ ✤ ❖ ✤ ❖ ✤ ❖ ✤ ❖ ✤ ❖ ✤ ❖ ✤ ❖ ✤ ❖ ✤ ❖ ✤ ❖ ✤ ❖ ✤ ❖ ✤ ❖

No other woman of Victorian Britain left her mark like Queen Victoria. She gave her name not only to the Victorian age but also to many places around the world, such as Victoria Falls in Africa. Statues and pictures of her appeared all over the **British Empire**. The queen had little real power, but her government (all men) listened to what she said with respect.

From princess to queen

Although born a princess, Victoria's life was like that of many other **upper-class** women. Her father died before she was a year old and she was brought up by her German mother. She did not go to school, but was taught by a **governess**. Lessons included learning to walk, head up, with a sprig of holly tied under her chin!

After Prince Albert died, Queen Victoria dressed in **mourning** black and kept her husband's room unchanged. This picture shows her in her old age.

Mother of the nation

People rarely saw Queen Victoria, but many admired her because she was dignified and 'respectable'. The royal family was held up as an example to all. Victoria's Jubilees of 1887 (50 years as queen) and 1897 (60 years) were celebrated with parades and bands all over the British Empire.

Victoria became queen in 1837, a month after her eighteenth birthday. She felt scared, but wrote in her diary that she promised to do her best. In 1840, she married her German cousin, Prince Albert. It was a happy marriage, and the couple had nine children. Queen Victoria became a grandmother when she was only 39.

The royal family

Victoria and Albert did not much like Buckingham Palace in London. It was too big, and its drains were bad. They preferred a smaller home called Osborne House on the Isle of Wight, where they lived quietly. They also enjoyed holidays in Scotland.

In 1861, Prince Albert died of the disease typhoid fever. The Queen was overcome with grief. She had come to rely on him, and took his advice on many matters. Now she was alone. She was only 43, but for the next 40 years she was the country's most famous **widow**.

Victoria's personal interests were her family, pets, riding, walking, drawing, music and writing letters. As queen, she took a close interest in her people, all over the British Empire. She was particularly pleased to be named Empress of India in 1876. She had two Indian manservants and, in 1887, wrote in her diary 'I am learning a few words of Hindustani to speak to my servants. It is a great interest to me…' Another pleasure, though often a worry, was her ever-growing family of grandchildren and great-grandchildren. Queen Elizabeth II is Victoria's great-great-granddaughter.

Women of the Empire

Women helped to run the **British Empire**. While living abroad, the wives of soldiers and colonial officials could do teaching, medical or **missionary** work. A young wife of an official often went with her husband if he was sent to foreign lands. Never having travelled far from home before, she might find herself on a steamship passing through the Suez Canal. Ahead lay India, Singapore or Australia. She might never return.

British women in India

Many British women went to live in India, where they tried to keep up a British way of life. They went horse racing, watched cricket matches, took tea and played cards. The wife of a British official or soldier often spent weeks on her own, while her husband was away visiting outlying districts or guarding the frontiers. Her children were looked after by an Indian nurse, called an *ayah*. It could be a lonely life, with few friends. British and Indian women did not often mix.

These emigrants are sailing for Australia. This picture shows unemployed needlewomen (seen left) travelling around the globe hoping for a better life. It was drawn in 1853.

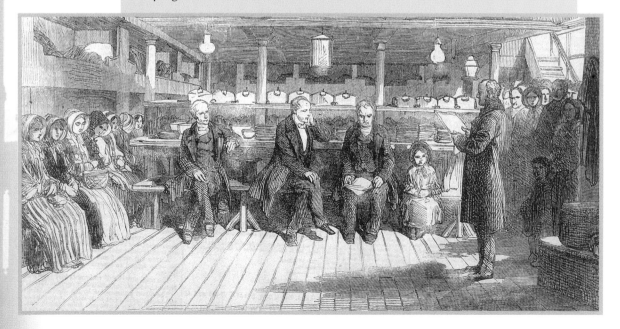

In 19th century Britain, women out-numbered men. Things were different in India, where there were 20 British men for every British woman. Ships from Britain arrived every year with single girls who had sailed East to find a husband.

Women making new lives

Other women left Britain as **emigrants**. Mostly with their families, but sometimes alone, women made long sea journeys to new lives in the USA, Canada, South Africa, Australia and New Zealand.

In the 1830s, the government encouraged young women from Britain to settle in Australia. How scared some newcomers must have been. Australia was much bigger and wilder than Britain; it was hot, dry and full of unfamiliar animals (including poisonous spiders and snakes). British women soon found their heavy clothing was not suited to Australia's climate.

In the bush or 'outback', home could be a shack known as a *humpie,* made from bark, branches and scraps of anything handy. Women fed their families on tea, roast mutton and flour-and-water bread baked in the ashes of a wood fire. The nearest doctor was often many miles away. Few **settlers** sought the help of the Aboriginal people, who knew the land much better than they did.

However, in spite of the difficulties, many women and their families settled successfully abroad in the end.

Helping women settle in Australia

Caroline Jones was a farmer's daughter who married a ship's captain named Archibald Chisholm. In India, Caroline started a school for soldiers' daughters. The Chisholms moved to Australia in 1838, and in 1841 Caroline opened a home for British girls arriving in Sydney. She made long trips by wagon with 'her girls', to make sure they safely reached the farms where she had arranged for them to live and work.

How do we know?

As we have seen in this book, Victorian women led lives that, in many ways, were very different from the way we live today. Fortunately, there is a lot of fascinating **evidence** available to help us learn more about them.

Victorian women in words and pictures

Many women left letters, diaries, books and drawings, describing their thoughts and details of their lives. Queen Victoria kept diaries all her life. So did some working women, such as Hannah Cullick. Florence Nightingale wrote hundreds of letters, as did many servant girls. Women also wrote for magazines and newspapers to argue for more rights. We can still read many of their articles today.

Museums recreate Victorian homes, shops and factories. The Beamish Museum in County Durham is an open-air museum where workers dress up in Victorian clothes and show everyday tasks as they would have been done. This woman is baking bread.

There are many pictures of Victorian women. Some Victorian painters pictured them as medieval princesses or Greek goddesses. Others showed ordinary women working in factories or on farms. These pictures show us colours, as old photos do not. The Victorian age was the first in history to leave us photographs, moving film and recordings of women's voices. Many families still have old photos of Victorian ancestors. Some of the photographers were women, including Julia Margaret Cameron, who was given her first camera as a present from her daughter.

Books

Some women wrote their own life-stories. In 1857, Mary Seacole wrote a book called *Wonderful Adventures of Mrs Seacole in Many Lands*, the only source we have about much of her life. Mary was born in Jamaica in 1805 but she travelled all the way from Jamaica to the Crimea to help wounded soldiers in the **Crimean War**. The other famous nurse who helped Crimean soldiers is Florence Nightingale. She became so famous that many books were written about her.

Official records

Since 1801, there has been a national **census** in Britain every ten years, providing new information on how women and other residents live. Yearly reports recording marriages, births and deaths show us the average age of newly married wives, for example. The average figures for 1884–85 show that miners' wives were 22, clerks' wives were 24, while the wives of 'professional and independent' men were 26. Inspectors reported on women's working conditions, too. One, in 1842, said that women toiling in factories had no time to 'make a shirt, darn a stocking, cook a dinner or clean a house'.

Things to see

All over Britain, there are places to visit which show what Victorian women's lives were like. In some country houses open to the public, you can see what a typical maid's room looked like, and compare it with the bedroom of the lady of the house. Many museums have 'Victoriana' (Victorian things) on display – items such as kitchen utensils, for example. All this evidence will help you to understand how Victorian women lived, and how they helped to shape the world in which we live today.

Timeline

1836	New law allows couples to marry in other churches besides the Church of England
1837	Victoria becomes queen
1840s	Queen Victoria marries Prince Albert. Start of mass **emigration** from Britain and Ireland to the USA, Australia, Canada and New Zealand
1842	New law stops women from working underground in coal mines
1847	First 'Ten-Hour Act' reduces working day for women and children aged under eighteen
1848	First training school for women teachers set up in London
1849	Walter Hunt invents the modern-style safety pin, soon popular with mothers for fastening nappies
1851	The Great Exhibition is held in London
1853–56	Crimean War
1859	Society for the Promotion of Employment for Women is founded
1861	Mrs Beeton publishes her *Book of Household Management* Prince Albert dies and Victoria goes into **mourning**
1870s	Prams and bottle-feeding become popular with mothers. **Typewriters** in offices are used by women workers
1882	Married Women's Property Act is passed. This gives married women, rather than their husbands, control over their own belongings.
1884	First public lavatory for women opens in London's Oxford Street
1887	Queen Victoria's Golden Jubilee (50 years as queen)
1889	Women's Franchise League founded to push for women getting the vote
1897	Queen Victoria celebrates her Diamond Jubilee (60 years as queen)
1901	Queen Victoria dies. Her eldest son becomes King Edward VII

Sources

Sources (selected)

British Women (Europa, 1983)
A Country Camera 1844–1914, Gordon Winter (Penguin, 1973)
Dickens' London, Peter Ackroyd (Headline, 1987)
Lark's Rise to Candleford, Flora Thompson (Penguin, 2000)
Oxford Illustrated History of Britain, ed. Kenneth O Morgan (OUP, 1984)
A Social and Economic History of Industrial Britain, John Robottom (Longman, 1986)
Victorian Things, Asa Briggs (Penguin, 1990)
Victorian Village Life, Neil Philip (Albion Press, 1993)
Willingly to School, Mary C Borer (Lutterworth, 1976)

Further reading

Victorian Factories, Andrew Langley, (Heinemann, 1996)
Victorian Britain, Andrew Langley, (Heinemann, 1994)

Also, look on www.heinemannexplore.co.uk for more information on the Victorians.

Places to visit

Bethnal Green Museum of Childhood, London
Castle Museum, York
Gunnersbury Park Museum, London (includes a reconstructed kitchen)
Museum of Childhood, Edinburgh
Museum of English Rural Life, Reading
Museum of London
New Lanark Visitor Centre, Lanark
North of England Open Air Museum, Beamish, Co Durham
Shugborough Estate, Stafford (restored estate)
Victoria and Albert Museum, London
Weald and Downland Museum, near Chichester, West Sussex
Welsh Folk Museum, St Fagans, Cardiff

Glossary

accounts records of money earned and money spent

Act law passed in parliament

boarding school school where children live in during term time

British Empire countries ruled by Britain or linked to it (from the late 17th century to the mid-20th century)

campaigner person who actively supports a cause or campaign, like a reformer

census official population count, collecting information about people

cholera a disease spread in water or crowded conditions

corset tight garment laced around the stomach, to draw in the waist

courtship when a man and woman go out together before marriage

craftworker skilled worker, often making things using hand-tools, such as a potter or dressmaker

Crimean War war in which Britain, France and Turkey fought against Russia (1853–56)

divorce legal ending of a marriage

emigrate/emigration to leave your home country to make a new life in another land

evidence writings, pictures or other proof that something happened

gadget equipment that does a job more easily or quickly

governess female private tutor, who lived with the children she taught

gramophone machine for playing recorded sounds on cylinders or discs

Industrial Revolution great changes in manufacturing and machinery beginning in the 1700s, but mainly taking place in Victorian times

journalism articles in magazines and newspapers

kitchen range large coal-burning stove for cooking and heating water

manager someone who oversees other people's work

matchmaking arranging a marriage by bringing two people together

Member of Parliament someone elected by people in an area to represent them in the government and help make laws

middle class social group made up of people in between those richer (upper class) and poorer (working class)

missionary someone who teaches their religion to people of other faiths, usually in another country

mourning period of sadness after someone dies

music hall popular theatre show of the late 1800s, with singers, dancers, comedians and other performers such as jugglers and magicians

nanny woman paid to look after someone else's children in their home

National Trust organization founded in 1895 to preserve areas of natural beauty and historic buildings

outcast person driven out of a community or on its fringes

parasol type of umbrella used to keep off the hot sun in summer

penny-farthing bicycle with a very large front wheel (the 'penny') and a much smaller back wheel (the 'farthing' – a small coin)

pension money paid to old and retired people

pioneer person who does something for the first time

reformer person who tries to change something to improve it

rent money paid by a person to live in a room, a flat or a house owned by someone else

revolution upheaval that changes a way of life or government

rights claims to fairer or equal treatment

sanitation clean and safe disposal of toilet waste

settler person making a permanent new home after travelling through a new land

slums poor areas of bad housing, lacking proper clean water

scullery small room with a sink, used for washing-up

socialism belief in the shared ownership of wealth and property

strike refusing to work, as part of a campaign for more money or better conditions

tiara small crown-like hairpiece, set with jewels

typewriter writing machine with keyboard widely used from the 1870s

typhus fever caught due to disease-carrying lice

widow/widowhood a woman whose husband has died; widowhood means 'being a widow'

women's rights demand for equal treatment for women such as the right to vote, own property or arrange their own domestic lives

working class social group of people who, in Victorian times, mostly worked as servants or in factories, for low wages

Index

Titles in the *Victorians* series are:

Hardback   0 431 14621 7

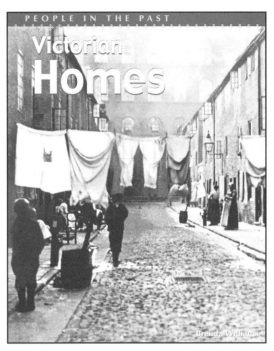

Hardback   0 431 14623 3

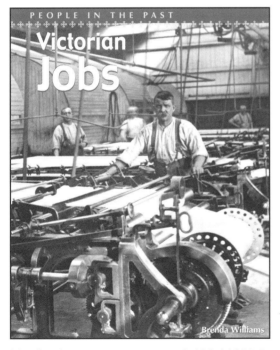

Hardback   0 431 14622 5

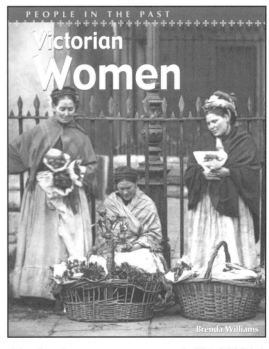

Hardback   0 431 14624 1

Find out about the other titles in this series on our website www.heinemann.co.uk/library